STARTING A VENDING MACHINE BUSINESS GUIDE

Step-by-Step Strategies to Build a Successful Full-Time Income on Autopilot with a Successful Vending Machine Business

(Complete Beginners' Guide)

PEDRO DURANT

Copyright © 2024 by Pedro Durant All rights reserved.

No part of this publication may be reproduced, distributed, or transmitted in any form or by any means, including photocopying, recording, or other electronic or mechanical methods, without the prior written permission of the author, except in the case of brief quotations embodied in critical reviews and certain other noncommercial uses permitted by copyright law.

First Edition: 2024

Disclaimer: The information provided in this book is for educational purposes only. The author and publisher make no representations or warranties with respect to the accuracy or completeness of the contents of this work. The advice and strategies contained herein may not be suitable for every situation. The author shall not be held liable for any damages arising from the use of this book.

CONTENTS

Introduction   3
- Welcome to Starting a Vending Machine Business Guide
- Why This Book Is Different
- A Business That Fits Your Life
- The Goal of This Book

Chapter 1: The Vending Machine Business Landscape   6
- Understanding the Vending Machine Market
- Key Trends in the Vending Machine Industry
- Why Now Is the Best Time to Start

Chapter 2: What Is a Vending Machine?   9
- What Do Vending Machines Do?
- Different Types of Vending Machines

Chapter 3: Why Start a Vending Machine Business?   14
- The Benefits of Vending Machines
- Understanding the Income Potential

Chapter 4: Building a Business Plan   20
- Setting Your Goals
- Market Research and Target Audience
- 3 Budget Planning and Financial Projections
- Scaling Your Vending Business

Chapter 5: Picking the Right Vending Machines   28
- Types of Vending Machines: Snack, Drink, Combination
- New vs. Used Machines
- Key Features to Look For in a Vending Machine

Chapter 6: Finding Good Locations   36
- What Makes a Good Location?
- How to Negotiate with Property Owners
- Real-Life Examples of Successful Locations

Chapter 7: Stocking and Managing Your Machines   44

- Choosing the Right Products for Your Market
- Restocking and Monitoring Inventory
- Maintaining Quality Control and Freshness

Chapter 8: Money Management and Growth   **50**
- Tracking Your Revenue and Expenses
- Reinvesting in Your Business
- Expanding Your Fleet of Machines

Chapter 9: Digital Marketing for Vending Machines   **57**
- Building an Online Presence for Your Business
- Social Media Marketing for Local Engagement
- SEO and Local Search Optimization
- Leveraging Email Marketing and Paid Ads

Chapter 10: Taking Care of Your Machines   **65**
- Regular Maintenance and Cleaning
- Troubleshooting Common Issues
- Upgrading and Modernizing Your Machines
- Handling Customer Issues and Refunds

Chapter 11: Rules, Regulations, and Compliance   **72**
- Permits and Licensing Requirements
- Health and Safety Regulations
- Insurance and Liability
- Staying Informed About Regulations

Chapter 12: Conclusion   **78**
- Recap of Key Point
- Preparing for Your Vending Journey
- Final Tips for Success
- Moving Forward

INTRODUCTION

Welcome to "**Starting a Vending Machine Business Guide**". your comprehensive roadmap to starting and growing a profitable vending machine business. This book will guide you through each step, from understanding the basics to managing your machines efficiently and scaling your business for long-term growth.

Vending machines are an excellent opportunity for generating passive income while maintaining flexibility in your schedule. Unlike many other business ventures, vending machines operate 24/7, generating revenue at all hours without needing constant attention. With the increasing demand for convenience, vending machines provide a practical solution, offering quick access to snacks, drinks, and even specialized items at locations where people need them most—like offices, schools, gyms, and public spaces.

The vending machine business is lucrative because it combines simplicity with a high potential for earnings. With relatively low startup costs and maintenance requirements, you can start small and expand as your business grows. Whether you're interested in managing a few machines locally or scaling up to operate multiple machines across different locations, this guide will
provide the insights and strategies you need to succeed.

Why This Book Is Different

Unlike many generic guides, this book provides actionable steps tailored to real-life challenges and opportunities within the vending machine industry. You'll gain insights from case studies of successful vending machine operators, receive practical tips, and learn strategies that help you make well-informed decisions.

By the time you've finished reading, you'll know how to:

- Choose the right vending machines for your business.
- Identify high-traffic locations to maximize earnings.
- Stock your machines with products that perform well.
- Manage budgeting and cash flow effectively.
- Take care of your machines and resolve common issues.
- Utilize digital marketing to promote your vending business And much more!

A Business That Fits Your Life

One of the biggest advantages of a vending machine business is flexibility. Whether you're starting this as a side hustle or aiming to make it your full-time occupation, the model can adapt to fit your lifestyle. Once your machines are set up and stocked, you can focus on monitoring and scaling the business without needing to be physically present every day. With automation tools and proper planning, your machines can almost run themselves, giving you the freedom to focus on growth and other priorities.

In addition, vending machines can cater to almost any market or location. From healthy snack options for gyms to sweet treats for office workers and students, you can customize your vending machines to suit different customer needs.

The Goal of This Book

This book is not just about starting a vending machine business—it's about building a sustainable, profitable enterprise that can grow with you. Whether your goal is to create additional income or manage a full-time business, this guide will provide you with the knowledge and confidence to make informed decisions and take action.

Every successful business starts with a well-thought-out plan. By following the steps and advice laid out in this guide, you'll be ready to embark on your journey into the world of vending machines, with a clear vision and actionable strategies.

Let's get started—you're about to take the first step toward financial independence and an exciting entrepreneurial venture!

CHAPTER 1:

THE VENDING MACHINE BUSINESS LANDSCAPE

The vending machine business is an evolving and adaptable market that has proven resilient even in the face of technological and economic shifts. Whether it's the rise of new payment methods, changes in consumer preferences, or the growing demand for convenience, vending machines have continuously found a place in the retail market. In this chapter, we explore the current landscape of the vending machine business, key trends shaping the industry, and why now is the perfect time to start your own vending machine business.

1.1 Understanding the Vending Machine Market

The vending machine market is a multi-billion-dollar industry with opportunities for newcomers to find a profitable niche. Vending machines are everywhere, from office buildings to schools, gyms, malls, and transit hubs. The convenience they offer is unmatched—anyone can access a snack, drink, or even an essential item at any time of the day.

According to industry studies, the global vending machine market is expected to grow significantly over the next few years. This growth is driven by factors like increased demand for convenience, healthier snacking options, and technology that makes transactions easier and more secure. Vending machines are no longer limited to just snacks and drinks; they now dispense everything from tech gadgets to health and hygiene products.

1.2 Key Trends in the Vending Machine Industry

1. **Cashless Payment Solutions:** With fewer consumers carrying cash, many vending machine operators have upgraded their machines to accept credit cards, debit cards, and mobile payments. This adaptation has not only increased sales but also allowed for a more seamless customer experience.

2. **Health-Conscious Product Offerings:** There is growing demand for healthy snack options, especially in schools, gyms, and offices. Vending machines offering nutritious products such as protein bars, fresh juices, and low-calorie snacks are gaining popularity, catering to customers who are mindful of their diet.

3. **Eco-Friendly Machines:** Many businesses are adopting eco-friendly vending machines that use less energy or even offer biodegradable packaging for their products. Environmentally-conscious practices are becoming an important factor in consumer decision-making.

4. **Diverse Product Range:** Beyond just food and drinks, the vending machine industry is expanding into new areas. Machines now sell items like electronics, health supplies, and even fresh meals, appealing to a broader range of customer needs.

5. **Remote Monitoring Technology:** Advanced vending machines now offer remote monitoring features, allowing operators to track sales, stock levels, and machine health from their smartphone or computer. This technology significantly improves operational efficiency and profitability.

1.3 Why Now Is the Best Time to Start

The vending machine industry offers a unique opportunity to build a flexible business with low operating costs. Here are some reasons why this is an ideal time to start your vending machine venture:

- **Increased Demand for Convenience:** Consumers are increasingly looking for convenient shopping options, and vending machines provide an easy solution. Whether at a gym, an office building, or a public transportation hub, customers appreciate being able to purchase what they need quickly and without interaction.

- **Scalable Business Model:** Vending machines offer a scalable model, allowing you to start small and grow your business over time. Once you've established a few successful locations, you can reinvest in additional machines and expand to new areas.

- **Low Barrier to Entry:** Compared to many other types of businesses, the startup costs for a vending machine business are relatively low. You don't need a storefront or employees to get started. With a small initial investment, you can launch your business and start generating revenue quickly.

- **Passive Income Potential:** Once set up, vending machines require minimal oversight. This means you can earn passive income while focusing on other pursuits or even maintaining a separate full-time job.

CHAPTER 2:

WHAT IS A VENDING MACHINE?

A vending machine is an automated retail system that dispenses products—such as snacks, drinks, or other goods—directly to customers without the need for human interaction. These machines allow customers to make purchases by inserting money, using a card, or even opting for mobile payment options. In return, the machine dispenses the selected item instantly. Vending machines are found in locations ranging from schools and offices to gyms and shopping centers, and they offer unparalleled convenience.

The business model behind vending machines is simple yet effective: they generate income around the clock without requiring staff, making them an appealing option for small business owners and large companies alike. But what exactly do vending machines do, and how do they operate?

2.1 What Do Vending Machines Do?

At their core, vending machines are like miniature self-service shops that operate autonomously. Customers can purchase products anytime, making vending machines a reliable source for quick snacks, drinks, or essential items. By inserting cash, swiping a card, or tapping a mobile payment system, customers can select an item and receive it instantly.

One of the reasons vending machines are so successful is because they meet a fundamental consumer need for instant gratification. In places like transit hubs, offices, schools, or gyms, vending machines provide a convenient solution for hunger, thirst, or a quick purchase of essential items.

From a business standpoint, vending machines work 24/7, generating passive income without the need for constant supervision. They are low-maintenance, making them ideal for entrepreneurs seeking an easy-to-manage, scalable business. Vending machines can also be customized to dispense a wide variety of products depending on the needs of your target audience.

2.2 Different Types of Vending Machines

To run a successful vending machine business, it's important to understand the different types of machines available and the markets they serve. Each type of vending machine is tailored to cater to specific consumer demands and locations.

1. **Snack Vending Machines:** These are the most common types and are stocked with items like chips, candy bars, cookies, nuts, and granola bars. They're often placed in high-traffic areas like schools, offices, and gyms, where people need easy access to snacks.

2. **Drink Vending Machines:** Drink vending machines offer a variety of beverages such as bottled water, soda, energy drinks, and juice. These machines are ideal for locations like gyms, hospitals, and office break rooms, as they provide convenient hydration. They often include refrigeration to keep drinks cold.

3. **Combination Vending Machines:** Combination machines are designed to sell both snacks and drinks. These machines are perfect for locations with limited space that still have high demand for both snacks and beverages, providing a one-stop solution for customers.

4. **Specialty Vending Machines:** Specialty machines offer unique items, ranging from electronics like phone chargers to hygiene products like face masks. They're often found in places like airports, gyms, and malls where customers have specific needs.

5. **Healthy Vending Machines:** As the demand for healthy eating increases, many vending machine operators have adapted by stocking items like protein bars, fresh fruit, yogurt, and low-sugar drinks. These machines are popular in schools, fitness centers, offices, and hospitals.

The Flexibility of Vending Machines

One major advantage of vending machines is their adaptability. As a business owner, you can choose different types of machines and operate them in environments that best suit your target audience. Whether your customers are office workers, students, gym-goers, or travelers, vending machines can be customized to meet their specific needs.

With a wide range of options, you can start with just one or two machines and expand your fleet as your business grows. Targeting diverse audiences will allow your business to grow steadily and adapt to changing consumer trends.

CHAPTER 3:

WHY START A VENDING MACHINE BUSINESS?

Vending machines represent one of the most accessible and scalable business opportunities for entrepreneurs of all experience levels. Whether you're looking for a side income or aspiring to build a full-fledged enterprise, vending machines offer flexibility, minimal overhead, and the potential for significant profits with relatively low upfront costs. This chapter will explore why starting a vending machine business is a smart move and the key benefits that make this industry so appealing.

3.1 The Benefits of Vending Machines

There are several reasons why starting a vending machine business is an attractive option for many entrepreneurs:

1. **Low Operating Costs**
   One of the main advantages of a vending machine business is that it requires minimal ongoing expenses compared to many other types of businesses. Once you've purchased your machine and stocked it, the operating costs are generally low. There's no need to hire employees to manage daily operations or rent a storefront, which keeps overhead costs low.
   The primary ongoing expenses will be purchasing inventory, maintaining the machines, and possibly paying commissions or rent for your vending locations.

2. Passive Income

    Vending machines work for you around the clock. They operate 24/7, meaning that even while you're asleep or busy with other activities, your machines can be generating revenue. This makes vending machines an excellent source of passive income. With the right strategy, a few well-placed machines can bring in steady profits with minimal time investment once they are set up.

3. Flexibility and Scalability

    One of the most attractive features of the vending machine business is its flexibility. You can start small with just one or two machines and gradually scale up as your business grows. This allows you to test different locations and strategies without committing significant capital upfront. As your profits increase, you can reinvest in additional machines or explore more lucrative locations, growing your business at your own pace.
    This flexibility extends to the types of products you can offer as well. Whether you want to sell snacks, drinks, healthy options, or specialty items, you can tailor your vending machines to meet market demands. The ability to experiment with different products and locations adds to the overall scalability of the business.

4. Minimal Time Commitment

    A vending machine business is perfect for individuals looking for a low-time commitment business model. Once your machines are placed and stocked, you'll only need to spend time restocking and maintaining them. Many vending machine owners find that they can manage multiple machines with just a few hours of work per week, making it an excellent option for those who have other jobs or commitments.

5. Location Independence
   Another great benefit of vending machines is their portability. If one location isn't performing as well as expected, you can move your machine to a better spot. The vending machine business doesn't tie you to one fixed location, giving you the freedom to adapt and reposition your machines as needed. Additionally, you can operate in multiple locations simultaneously, giving you the chance to serve diverse markets.

6. Low Barrier to Entry
   Unlike other businesses that require substantial upfront capital or specialized knowledge, starting a vending machine business has a relatively low barrier to entry. With a small investment, you can purchase your first machine and begin generating revenue. No special licenses or certifications are usually required, making it accessible to entrepreneurs of all backgrounds.

3.2 Understanding the Income Potential

The income potential of a vending machine business depends on several factors, including location, product selection, and machine maintenance. However, many operators find that a well-placed machine can generate steady profits with minimal effort.

1. Earnings Based on Location
   The key factor that determines how much money a vending machine makes is location. High-traffic areas such as office buildings, schools, gyms, hospitals, and transit hubs provide

a steady stream of potential customers. Machines in these locations can generate hundreds or even thousands of dollars in revenue per month.

For example, a vending machine in a busy office building may serve employees who rely on snacks and drinks during their work breaks, resulting in regular sales throughout the day. Similarly, a machine in a gym can cater to fitness enthusiasts looking for healthy snacks or sports drinks after their workout, providing consistent income.

2. Product Selection

   Choosing the right products for your machine is crucial for maximizing sales. Offering popular snacks, drinks, or specialty items tailored to your location's demographics ensures that your machine attracts more customers. For instance, a vending machine in a gym may perform better if stocked with protein bars, bottled water, and energy drinks, while a machine in a school might need a variety of snacks appealing to students. Regularly reviewing sales data and adjusting your product offerings based on customer preferences is key to keeping your vending machine profitable. Additionally, offering seasonal or limited-time products can keep customers coming back for new options.

3. Profit Margins

   The profit margins in the vending machine business can be very appealing. While exact profit margins will vary depending on product costs and sales volume, vending machines typically have a high markup on the items they sell. For example, a bag of chips purchased for $0.50 might sell for $1.25, providing a significant return on investment. Bulk purchasing and sourcing products from wholesalers can further increase your profit margins. On average, vending machines can achieve a profit margin of 30-50%, making them a highly lucrative business when managed correctly.

4. **Multiple Machines, Multiple Streams of Income**
   As you gain experience in the vending machine business and find successful locations, you can scale up by adding more machines. With multiple machines in different locations, you create multiple streams of income, all contributing to your overall revenue. Many successful vending machine operators manage a fleet of machines across various high-traffic areas, allowing them to increase their earnings without significantly increasing their workload.

5. **Long-Term Growth Potential**
   Vending machines offer significant long-term growth potential. Once you've established a profitable business with a few machines, you can reinvest your earnings into expanding your machine network, upgrading to modern machines with more advanced features, or diversifying your product offerings. This steady growth model allows you to build a sustainable business over time.

The Versatility of the Business

Vending machines offer exceptional versatility. You can tailor your business to fit almost any market segment or consumer demographic. This adaptability is one of the reasons the vending machine industry continues to grow, and it makes the business particularly resilient to changing consumer trends.

Whether you're passionate about healthy living and want to focus on nutritious snacks, or you see a gap in the market for specialty vending products (such as hygiene products in a gym or office space), vending machines allow you to align your business with your passions and the needs of your customers.

CHAPTER 4:

BUILDING A BUSINESS PLAN

A strong business plan is the foundation of any successful vending machine business. It will guide your decisions, set clear objectives, and help you manage your finances as you grow your business.
A well-crafted business plan ensures that you have a roadmap to follow, helping you stay focused on your goals and adapt to challenges along the way.

4.1 Setting Your Goals

Before diving into the specifics of your vending machine business, it's essential to set clear, measurable goals. Having well-defined objectives will keep you motivated and allow you to track your progress. Here are some key areas to consider when setting your business goals:

1. **Income Targets**
   Determine how much revenue you want your vending machine business to generate. Your income goals will depend on whether you're starting the business as a side hustle or aiming to make it your full-time income. For example:

   > o **Short-term goal (First 6 months):** Generate $1,000 in monthly revenue with one to two machines.

   > o **Mid-term goal (1 year):** Expand your business to 5-7 machines and achieve $3,000-$5,000 in monthly revenue.

- **Long-term goal (3-5 years):** Operate a fleet of 15-20 machines in high-traffic locations, generating a full-time income of $10,000+ per month.

2. By setting these income targets, you'll have a clearer idea of how many machines you need, what kind of locations to target, and how to manage your finances.

3. Expansion and Scaling
Define how you plan to scale your business over time. Will you expand gradually by reinvesting profits, or do you intend to take out loans or seek investors to grow more rapidly? It's crucial to know how quickly you want to scale and what resources you'll need for growth. Here's how you can structure your scaling plan:

    - **Year 1:** Focus on learning the business, establishing a few successful locations, and refining your product offerings.

    - **Year 2:** Begin expanding by adding more machines to new locations. Look for opportunities to diversify the types of machines you operate (snack machines, healthy vending machines, etc.).

    - **Year 3 and beyond:** Manage a larger network of
    - machines across different markets, hire employees for maintenance and restocking, and explore automation tools for inventory management.

4. Customer Satisfaction
Set goals for customer satisfaction, which will ultimately drive repeat sales and positive word of mouth. For example, ensuring

that machines are always well-stocked, offering popular products, and keeping machines clean and functional are all critical aspects of a positive customer experience.

5. Building Brand Recognition
   If you want to grow a recognizable brand, your goals should include creating a consistent brand identity across your machines. This could include custom branding on the machines, a website, social media presence, and even offering loyalty programs for frequent users. Clear branding helps build trust and can make your machines stand out from the competition.

4.2 Market Research and Target Audience

Market research is a critical component of your business plan. Understanding the vending machine industry and identifying your target audience will help you make informed decisions about product selection, pricing, and locations.

1. Industry Overview
   Research the overall vending machine industry in your area. Learn about current trends, such as the growing demand for healthy vending machines or eco-friendly options, and assess how much competition exists in your market. Understanding these trends will help you position your business strategically.

2. Identifying Your Target Audience
   Your target audience will largely depend on the locations you choose for your vending machines. Here are a few examples of different target audiences and the kinds of products they're likely to purchase:

o **Office workers:** They typically look for convenient snacks and beverages to fuel their workday, such as coffee, bottled water, soda, chips, and candy bars.

o **Students:** At schools and universities, students might prefer affordable snacks, drinks, and even meal replacements. Healthier options can be a good fit here due to growing awareness of nutrition.

o **Gym-goers:** Fitness enthusiasts are often interested in energy bars, protein shakes, bottled water, and other products that support their active lifestyle.

o **Travelers:** Vending machines in airports, train stations, or bus terminals might focus on drinks, snacks, travel essentials (such as hygiene products), and electronics (chargers, earphones, etc.).

3. Knowing your target audience allows you to stock your machines with products that will sell quickly, maximizing your revenue potential. Tailoring your offerings to the specific needs of your customers in each location is essential for success.

4. Analyzing Competitors
    Assess your competition by studying other vending machines in your area. What kinds of products are they selling? How often do they restock their machines? Is there an opportunity to offer something different, such as healthier options, more competitive prices, or better product variety?
    Use this analysis to differentiate your business from your

competitors. For example, if most machines in a particular location offer junk food, you could stand out by offering healthy snacks and beverages. Alternatively, you could focus on providing better service, such as restocking more frequently or ensuring that your machines accept the latest payment methods.

5. Conducting Surveys and Research

You can further refine your market research by conducting surveys with potential customers in your target locations. Ask them what kinds of products they'd like to see in a vending machine or what would make them more likely to use one. Gathering feedback from your target audience is invaluable for shaping your product offerings and pricing strategy.

4.3 Budget Planning and Financial Projections

Budgeting is one of the most important aspects of building a successful vending machine business. You'll need to carefully plan your finances, from the initial investment to ongoing expenses, to ensure that your business remains profitable.

1. Initial Investment

    Your upfront costs will include purchasing vending machines, stocking products, and possibly paying for location fees or commissions to property owners. Here's a breakdown of potential startup costs:

    o **Cost of vending machines:** Depending on whether you're buying new or used, machines can range from $1,500 to $10,000 per machine.

    o **Stocking products:** Your first stock purchase will depend on the types of products you're offering. For example, stocking a snack machine could cost $300-$500 initially.

- o **Transportation and setup:** You may need to pay for transporting the machine to its location and setting it up, especially if it's a large or refrigerated machine.

- o **Permits and licenses:** Some areas require vending machine licenses or permits, which can cost anywhere from $50 to $200 annually.

2. **Operating Expenses**
Once your machine is up and running, there will be ongoing costs to consider:

- o **Restocking products:** The cost of restocking your machine will depend on how frequently your products sell and the prices you've set.

- o **Maintenance and repairs:** While vending machines are generally low-maintenance, you'll occasionally need to repair or service them to keep them in good working order.

- o **Commissions or rental fees:** Many locations will charge you a commission on sales (usually around 5-20%) or a flat rental fee for placing your vending machine on their property. Be sure to account for these costs in your budget.

3. **Revenue Projections**
Your revenue projections should be based on realistic estimates of product sales and average foot traffic at your vending machine

locations. Start by calculating how much revenue one machine can generate per month, and scale this based on the number of machines you plan to operate.

Here's an example:
- o **Daily sales per machine:** $30 (assuming an average of 20 customers spending $1.50 each)
- o **Monthly sales:** $30 x 30 days = $900
- o **Number of machines:** 3
- o **Total monthly sales:** $900 x 3 = $2,700

4. Factor in your expenses and determine your profit margins to estimate your net income. As you expand, your revenue projections will increase based on the number of machines you add and how effectively you manage them.

4.4 Scaling Your Vending Business

As you grow your vending machine business, scalability should be a core focus. Scaling allows you to increase your revenue without dramatically increasing your workload.

1. **Reinvesting Profits**
A good rule of thumb is to reinvest a portion of your profits into growing your business. For example, you can use profits from one or two machines to purchase additional machines and expand into new locations. Reinvesting consistently will help you build a larger fleet of machines over time.

2. **Diversifying Your Machine Fleet**
To reduce risk and increase profitability, consider diversifying your vending machine offerings. For instance, you might start with traditional snack and drink machines and later expand

into healthy vending machines, specialty machines, or even those that offer unique items like electronics or hygiene products. Diversification helps you cater to different markets and consumer demands.

3. **Automating Inventory and Maintenance**
    As your business grows, managing multiple machines can become time-consuming. Consider using software or apps that help you track inventory, monitor sales, and schedule restocking visits. These tools can automate many of the operational tasks associated with your business, freeing up time for you to focus on expanding your business further.

CHAPTER 5:

PICKING THE RIGHT VENDING MACHINES

Choosing the right vending machines is one of the most critical decisions you'll make in your business. The type of machine you select will impact your initial investment, the products you can offer, and the long-term success of your business. In this chapter, we'll explore the different types of vending machines, the pros and cons of new versus used machines, and the key features to look for when making your purchase.

5.1 Types of Vending Machines: Snack, Drink, Combination

Understanding the various types of vending machines will help you determine which is the best fit for your business model and the locations you plan to target. Here's a breakdown of the most common types of vending machines:

1. **Snack Vending Machines**
   Snack vending machines are the most common type and are found in many locations, including schools, offices, gyms, and public spaces. These machines offer a wide range of snacks such as chips, candy, granola bars, nuts, and even healthier options like dried fruit or yogurt-covered snacks.
   Pros:
   o High demand for snack items in various locations.
   o Wide range of product options to appeal to different customer preferences.
   o Easy to restock with bulk snack items.

Cons:
- Snacks have a limited shelf life, requiring regular restocking to maintain freshness.
- Some locations may require healthier options due to regulations, which can be more expensive to stock.

2. **Drink Vending Machines**

   Drink vending machines offer a selection of beverages such as bottled water, soda, energy drinks, juices, and sometimes coffee. Many drink vending machines are refrigerated to keep beverages cold, making them a popular option in locations like gyms, offices, and public transportation hubs.

   Pros:
   - Beverages are high-margin products with consistent demand.
   - Refrigeration ensures that products stay fresh longer than snacks.
   - Machines are relatively low-maintenance once stocked.

   Cons:
   - Refrigerated machines consume more electricity, increasing operational costs.
   - The size and weight of beverage bottles can make restocking more physically demanding.
   - Some drinks, such as sodas, may be restricted in schools or certain health-conscious locations.

3. **Combination Vending Machine**

   Combination vending machines offer both snacks and drinks, making them an excellent choice for locations where space is limited but demand is high. These machines combine the functionality of both a snack and a drink machine in one, offering a greater variety of products to customers.

Pros:
- o Offer both food and drink options, increasing potential sales from one machine.
- o Ideal for smaller locations that cannot accommodate multiple machines.
- o Customers appreciate the convenience of getting both snacks and drinks from a single machine.

Cons:
- o Combination machines may have less storage capacity for each product type, requiring more frequent restocking.
- o They are more expensive than single-purpose machines, increasing the initial investment cost.

4. **Specialty Vending Machines**

Specialty vending machines are designed to dispense non traditional items such as hygiene products, electronics (like phone chargers or headphones), or even freshly brewed coffee. These machines are often found in airports, gyms, shopping malls, and other locations where customers need convenience items on the go.

Pros:
- o Unique product offerings allow you to stand out from traditional vending machines.
- o Higher-priced items like electronics can offer larger profit margins.
- o Specialty machines can be tailored to niche markets, creating opportunities in less saturated locations.

Cons:
- o More complex machines often come with higher maintenance requirements and costs.

o Product turnover may be slower, as specialty items are not purchased as frequently as snacks or drinks.
o You may need to work closely with suppliers to ensure you always have the right products in stock.

5. Healthy Vending Machines

Healthy vending machines are a growing trend, especially in schools, gyms, and offices. These machines offer nutritious snacks and beverages like protein bars, low-sugar drinks, fruit cups, and other health-conscious options.

Pros:

o Increasing consumer demand for healthier options makes this a lucrative niche.
o Schools and workplaces are often required to offer healthier food choices, creating more opportunities.
o You can charge premium prices for health-focused products, increasing profit margins.

Cons:

o Healthier snacks and drinks are often more expensive to purchase in bulk, increasing your upfront costs.
o Some locations may have low demand for healthy products, leading to slower sales.

5.2 New vs. Used Machines

Once you've decided on the type of vending machine you want, the next step is determining whether to purchase new or used machines. Both options have their advantages and disadvantages, so it's essential to weigh your budget and long-term goals before making a decision.

Buying New Machines

New vending machines come with the latest technology, warranties, and modern payment options (such as card readers and mobile payments). They are generally more reliable and less likely to break down, making them a good investment for entrepreneurs who want a hassle-free experience.

    Pros:

- **Warranty coverage:** Most new machines come with a warranty, giving you peace of mind in case something goes wrong.
- **Advanced features:** New machines often come with built-in card readers, mobile payment options (like Apple Pay or Google Pay), and inventory tracking software.
- **Energy efficiency:** New machines tend to be more energy-efficient, reducing electricity costs, especially for refrigerated drink machines.

    Cons:

- **Higher upfront cost:** New machines can cost anywhere from $3,000 to $10,000, depending on the type and features.
- **Slower return on investment:** The higher initial cost means it will take longer to recoup your investment, particularly if you're just starting out.

Buying Used Machines

Used vending machines are a cost-effective option for entrepreneurs with a smaller budget. You can often find high-quality used machines at a fraction of the cost of new ones, allowing you to start your business with less capital. However, buying used machines comes with some risks, as they may require repairs or lack modern payment features.

Pros:
- **Lower upfront cost:** Used machines are significantly cheaper than new ones, often costing between $1,000 and $3,000, depending on their age and condition.
- **Faster return on investment:** With a lower initial cost, you can achieve profitability more quickly.
- **Availability:** There is a large market for used vending machines, giving you plenty of options to choose from.

Cons:
- **Lack of warranty:** Used machines usually don't come with a warranty, meaning you'll need to cover any repair or maintenance costs yourself.
- **Outdated technology:** Some used machines may not have modern features like credit card readers or mobile payment options, limiting your payment flexibility.
- **Potential for higher maintenance costs:** Older machines may require more frequent repairs and upkeep, eating into your profits.

5.3 Key Features to Look For in a Vending Machine

When purchasing a vending machine, there are several essential features to consider. These features can impact both the customer experience and your operational efficiency, so it's crucial to choose wisely.

1. **Payment Options**
   As more consumers move away from cash, offering a variety of payment options is essential for maximizing sales. Look for machines that accept:
   - **Cash:** While becoming less common, cash payments are still used by some customers.

o **Credit and debit cards:** Machines equipped with card readers are a must in today's cashless society.
o **Mobile payments:** Many new machines offer mobile payment options like Apple Pay, Google Wallet, and contactless cards, making transactions quick and easy for customers.

2. Energy Efficiency

Energy-efficient vending machines are particularly important if you're operating drink machines or refrigerated units, as these consume more power. Look for machines with energy-saving features, such as LED lighting, low-energy compressors, or timers that reduce power consumption during off-peak hours. These features will help lower your operating costs over time.

3. Product Capacity

The size and capacity of the machine will depend on the location and the types of products you're selling. Machines with larger capacities will require less frequent restocking, reducing the time you spend maintaining them. Make sure the machine has enough space for a wide variety of products while still fitting comfortably in your chosen location.

4. User-Friendly Design

A user-friendly design is essential for ensuring a positive customer experience. Machines should have clear displays, intuitive buttons or touchscreens, and easily accessible payment options. Machines that are difficult to use can frustrate customers, leading to fewer sales.

5. Remote Monitoring and Inventory Tracking

Many modern vending machines come equipped with

inventory tracking and remote monitoring software. These systems allow you to check stock levels, sales data, and potential issues in real-time from your computer or smartphone. This feature can save you time and money by letting you know when it's time to restock or when a machine requires maintenance, eliminating unnecessary trips to the machine.

CHAPTER 6:

FINDING GOOD LOCATIONS

The location of your vending machine can make or break your business. A well-placed vending machine in a high-traffic, high demand area can generate consistent revenue with minimal effort, while a poorly placed machine can result in low sales and wasted investment. In this chapter, we'll explore the key factors to consider when selecting a location, how to approach property owners, and real-life examples of successful vending machine placements.

6.1 What Makes a Good Location?

When evaluating potential locations for your vending machine, there are several critical factors to consider. Each of these will play a significant role in determining how successful your machine will be.

1. Foot Traffic
   Foot traffic is one of the most important factors in finding a successful vending machine location. The more people passing by your machine, the higher the likelihood of sales. Locations with high foot traffic, such as busy office buildings, schools, gyms, hospitals, and transit stations, provide an ample customer base for your vending machine. However, simply having foot traffic isn't enough—you need to ensure that the people passing by have a reason to purchase from your machine.

2. Customer Need

   Identifying customer needs is critical. Your vending machine must offer products that are relevant and useful to the people frequenting the location. For example:

   o **Office buildings:** Employees may need quick snacks and drinks during the workday.
   o **Gyms:** Fitness enthusiasts often prefer healthy options like protein bars, bottled water, and energy drinks.
   o **Schools:** Students look for affordable snacks during breaks.
   o **Hospitals:** Staff and visitors may need snacks and drinks after cafeteria hours, or even small hygiene items from specialty machines.

   Understanding the needs of the people who frequent the location will help you choose the right products and increase your sales potential.

3. Competition

   It's important to assess the competition in any location you're considering. If there are already several vending machines in the area offering the same products, it may be more challenging to carve out a profitable niche. However, competition isn't always a dealbreaker—if you can offer superior product selection, healthier options, or more convenient payment methods, you can still succeed.

   Additionally, consider what other food or drink options are available in the area. For example, if your vending machine is in a location where there's a cafeteria or nearby snack shop, you may need to offer more competitive pricing or unique products to attract customers.

4. Security and Accessibility

    Security is an important consideration when choosing a location for your vending machine. Machines placed in secure, well-monitored areas are less likely to be vandalized or tampered with. Office buildings, schools, gyms, and corporate campuses tend to be safer locations for vending machines, while public transportation hubs or outdoor areas may require more robust security features (such as cameras or tamper-proof locks).

    In addition to security, the machine needs to be easily accessible to customers. It should be placed in a visible, convenient spot where people can quickly access it without any obstacles. For example, in an office building, placing the machine near the break room or lobby will encourage more use than if it's tucked away in a corner.

5. Operating Hours

    Some locations, like office buildings or schools, may have limited operating hours, which can restrict the time people have to use your vending machine. On the other hand, locations like gyms, hospitals, and transportation hubs are typically open 24/7, allowing your machine to generate revenue around the clock. Consider how the operating hours of your chosen location will affect sales volume.

6.2 How to Negotiate with Property Owners

Once you've identified a prime location for your vending machine, the next step is to negotiate with the property owner or manager. In most cases, you'll need to get permission to place your machine on their property, and you may need to offer them a commission or pay a rental fee.

1. Present the Benefits
   When approaching property owners or managers, it's important to emphasize the benefits of having a vending machine on their premises. Here are a few key selling points:
      - **Convenience for employees or customers:** A vending machine provides easy access to snacks and drinks without the need to leave the building or wait for a store to open.
      - **Revenue-sharing opportunities:** Many property owners are willing to host vending machines in exchange for a percentage of the sales. Offering a commission (typically between 5-20% of sales) can make the arrangement more appealing.
      - **Low maintenance for the property owner:** Assure them that you'll handle all aspects of stocking, cleaning, and maintaining the machine, so they won't have to worry about any additional responsibilities.

2. Be Prepared with Numbers
   Property owners will want to know how your vending machine will benefit them financially. Be prepared to provide a rough estimate of how much revenue the machine is likely to generate and what percentage of the profits they can expect to receive. For example:
      - If you project that your machine will generate $1,000 per month, and you're offering a 10% commission, the property owner could expect to earn $100 per month from hosting the machine.

3. Offer Flexibility
   Be open to negotiating the terms of the arrangement. Some property owners may prefer a flat rental fee instead of a

percentage of sales, while others might want to renegotiate after a trial period to assess the machine's performance. Flexibility and a willingness to find a mutually beneficial solution can increase your
chances of securing the location.

4. **Provide a Trial Period**
   If a property owner is hesitant to agree to a long-term arrangement, offer them a trial period (e.g., 3-6 months) to test the machine's performance. During this time, both you and the property owner can assess whether the vending machine is generating enough sales to justify keeping it in place. This approach lowers the risk for the property owner and gives you an opportunity to prove the value of the machine.

5. **Address Concerns**
   Be prepared to address any concerns the property owner may have, such as:
   - **Security:** Reassure them that your machine has anti-tamper features and that you'll regularly monitor it.
   - **Appearance:** Some property owners may be concerned about the aesthetics of a vending machine. You can offer to provide a modern, sleek design that fits the building's decor.
   - **Maintenance:** Let them know that you'll handle all maintenance and restocking, ensuring the machine is always clean and operational.

6.3 Real-Life Examples of Successful Locations

To give you an idea of how location impacts vending machine success, here are a few real-life examples of profitable locations:

1. Office Buildings

   Office buildings are prime locations for vending machines, especially in busy corporate environments where employees work long hours and often need convenient access to snacks and drinks. A well-stocked machine in an office building can generate significant revenue, particularly if it offers a variety of options, including coffee, energy drinks, and healthier snacks for health conscious employees.

   Example: A vending machine placed in a high-rise office building in downtown New York generated an average of $1,500 per month by catering to office workers who didn't have time to leave the building during their lunch breaks. The machine offered both snacks and drinks, with popular items including bottled water, energy bars, and granola.

2. Schools and Colleges

   Schools and colleges provide a captive audience of students who often need snacks and beverages between classes. Vending machines in these environments can be incredibly profitable, especially if they offer affordable and appealing snacks to students. Example: A vending machine placed in a community college in

California generated $1,200 per month. The machine was located near the
student lounge and offered a mix of
affordable snacks, candy, and drinks. The operator found that restocking the machine with
healthier options during exam periods (such as granola bars and bottled water) helped boost sales.

3. Gyms and Fitness Centers

   Gyms are ideal locations for vending machines that offer health-focused products like protein bars, energy drinks, and bottled water. Gym-goers often need quick access to hydration and post-workout snacks, making vending machines a convenient option. Example: A vending machine in a high-traffic gym in Atlanta generated $1,000 per month by offering protein bars, bottled water, and low-sugar  energy drinks. The machine was strategically placed near the locker rooms, ensuring it was easily accessible to gym-goers as they finished their workouts.

4. Hospitals

   Hospitals are another excellent location for vending machines, as they serve a wide range of people,
   including patients, visitors, and
   hospital staff. Vending machines in hospitals often operate 24/7,

providing much-needed convenience, especially during off-hours when cafeterias are closed.

Example: A vending machine placed in a hospital waiting room in Chicago generated an average of $2,000 per month. The machine offered a range of snacks, drinks, and small hygiene items (such as hand sanitizer and tissues), catering to both hospital staff and visitors.

5. Transportation Hubs

   Bus stations, train stations, and airports are high-traffic areas where travelers often need quick access to snacks, drinks, and travel essentials. Vending machines in these locations can be highly profitable, especially if they offer a mix of food, beverages, and small convenience items like phone chargers or earphones.

   Example: A vending machine placed in a busy train station in Lodon generated $2,500 per month by offering a mix of snacks, drinks, and travel essentials like phone chargers and earplugs. The machine was strategically placed near the waiting area, making it easily accessible to travelers on the go.

CHAPTER 7:

STOCKING AND MANAGING YOUR MACHINES

Once you've secured the right locations for your vending machines, the next crucial step is to stock them with the right products and manage them efficiently. Stocking and managing your vending machines well will help ensure steady sales and maximize your profits. In this chapter, we'll explore how to choose the right products, create an efficient restocking schedule, and maintain product quality to keep your customers satisfied.

7.1 Choosing the Right Products for Your Market

Selecting the right products to stock in your vending machines is key to driving sales. The products you choose should align with the preferences and needs of the customers at each location. When deciding what to stock, consider your target audience, the time of day they are most likely to make a purchase, and their specific needs.

1. Know Your Audience
   Each location will have a different demographic, and the products that appeal to office workers may differ significantly from what gym-goers or students prefer. Here's a breakdown of common vending machine locations and the products that tend to perform well in each:

   o **Office Buildings:** Office workers tend to favor snacks that are easy to eat on the go, such as chips, granola bars, candy bars, and bottled drinks like water, coffee, and soda. Healthier snack options (e.g., nuts, dried fruit, protein bars) are also in demand, especially in more corporate settings.

o **Schools and Colleges:** Students typically look for affordable, quick snacks like chips, candy, energy drinks, and bottled water. However, with the growing demand for healthier options in school environments, adding nutritious choices like trail mix, fruit cups, or low-sugar beverages can be beneficial.

o **Gyms:** Gym-goers prefer health-focused options like protein bars, energy drinks, electrolyte-replenishing sports drinks, and bottled water. Offering low-sugar, high-protein snacks that cater to people's fitness needs can increase your sales in fitness centers.

o **Hospitals:** Hospital vending machines serve a diverse customer base of patients, visitors, and medical staff. Popular products include bottled water, juice, snacks (chips, crackers, granola bars), and even small hygiene items like hand sanitizers and tissues.

o **Transportation Hubs:** In busy places like train stations or airports, travelers are often looking for quick, portable snacks and drinks to enjoy on the go. Items such as bottled water, soda, chips, candy, and grab-and-go sandwiches can sell well. Additionally, offering travel essentials like phone chargers, earbuds, or hand sanitizers may set your machine apart.

2. Monitor Trends

It's essential to stay up to date on consumer trends and preferences. For example, as more people become health conscious, the demand for healthier snacks and beverages is rising.

Offering a mix of traditional vending machine staples (like chips and soda) alongside healthier alternatives (like granola bars, dried fruit, and coconut water) will appeal to a broader range of customers.

If you notice a shift in what customers are purchasing, adjust your product offerings accordingly. Seasonal products, such as cold drinks in the summer or hot chocolate in the winter, can also drive additional sales during peak periods.

3. Price Sensitivity

   Customers in different locations will have varying levels of price sensitivity. For instance, students may prefer more affordable snacks, while corporate workers or gym-goers may be willing to pay a premium for healthier or higher-quality items. Research your target market and adjust your pricing strategy to maximize both sales and profit margins.

7.2 Restocking and Monitoring Inventory

Efficient restocking is crucial to maintaining your vending machine's profitability. Empty or poorly stocked machines frustrate customers and result in lost sales. Here's how to develop an effective restocking schedule and manage your inventory efficiently.

1. Create a Regular Restocking Schedule

   The frequency with which you restock your vending machines will depend on how fast your products sell and the type of location. High-traffic locations like busy office buildings, schools, or gyms may require restocking every few days, while lower-traffic areas may only need weekly or bi-weekly restocking.

Here are a few tips for maintaining an effective restocking schedule:

- o **Track sales data:** Keep detailed records of how often each item sells and how quickly your machines run out of stock. This will help you determine the ideal restocking frequency for each machine.
- o **Peak periods:** Consider restocking more frequently during peak sales periods. For example, if your machine is in a school, expect higher sales during the school year and lower sales during summer breaks.
- o **Plan routes efficiently:** If you operate multiple machines, plan your restocking routes efficiently to save time and reduce transportation costs. Group machines that are in close proximity and restock them in one trip.

2. Use Inventory Management Tools

   Tracking inventory levels manually can be time-consuming, especially if you operate several machines. Many modern vending machines come equipped with inventory tracking software that allows you to monitor stock levels remotely. With these tools, you can see which products are selling the fastest and which machines need restocking, allowing you to manage your machines more efficiently.

   For machines that don't have built-in tracking software, you can use spreadsheets or inventory management apps to track stock levels and sales.

3. Prevent Stockouts

   Stockouts—when a vending machine runs out of products—can lead to lost sales and dissatisfied customers. To avoid this, monitor your inventory levels closely and plan restocking visits before your machine runs low. Set a minimum stock level for each product (for example, when only 20% of the stock remains) and plan to restock before reaching that point.

4. Rotating Inventory

   To keep customers interested and encourage repeat sales, rotate your inventory periodically. Introduce new products, seasonal items, or limited-time offers to give customers a reason to keep coming back to your machine. You can also use sales data to identify underperforming products and replace them with more popular options.

7.3 Maintaining Quality Control and Freshness

Quality control is a crucial aspect of managing your vending machine business. Customers expect the products in your machines to be fresh, and a machine stocked with expired or stale items will damage your reputation and reduce sales.

1. Monitor Expiration Dates

   It's essential to regularly check the expiration dates on all products in your machines. Make a habit of reviewing expiration dates during each restocking visit, removing any items that are close to expiring. Not only does this ensure that your customers receive fresh products, but it also protects you from any potential liability associated with selling expired goods.

2. Keep Machines Clean

   A clean vending machine attracts more customers. Wipe down the exterior of your machines during restocking visits to remove dust, fingerprints, and spills. Clean the inside of the machine periodically to ensure that the dispensing mechanisms are free from debris, and keep any refrigerated compartments well-maintained to avoid spoilage.

3. Maintain Temperature Control

    If you're operating drink machines or machines that contain perishable items (such as sandwiches or yogurt), maintaining proper temperature control is essential. Ensure that the refrigeration system is functioning correctly to keep products fresh. You may need to check and adjust the temperature settings based on seasonal changes.

4. Handling Complaints and Refunds

    Even with the best management practices, issues can arise, such as products getting stuck or machines malfunctioning. It's essential to provide customers with a simple way to report problems and request refunds. Post clear contact information on your machine (e.g., phone number or email) where customers can reach you if they encounter issues. Respond to complaints promptly and offer refunds or replacements to maintain customer satisfaction.

CHAPTER 8:

MONEY MANAGEMENT AND GROWTH

Proper money management is crucial to running a profitable vending machine business. While the business model is relatively simple, staying on top of your finances ensures you maximize your profits and avoid potential pitfalls. In this chapter, we'll explore how to track revenue and expenses, reinvest your profits wisely, and scale your business over time.

8.1 Tracking Your Revenue and Expenses

To build a sustainable vending machine business, it's essential to track your revenue and expenses accurately. This helps you assess the profitability of each machine, identify trends, and make informed decisions about how to optimize your operations.

1. **Recording Sales**
   Start by keeping detailed records of your vending machine sales. Each time you restock a machine, note how much inventory was sold and calculate the total revenue generated. You can track sales manually using spreadsheets, or if your machine is equipped with inventory tracking software, you can automate this process.
   Here's an example of what to track:

   - **Items sold:** Track how many of each item is sold between restocking visits.

o **Total sales:** Multiply the number of items sold by the price of each item to calculate total revenue.
o **Average daily sales:** Divide total sales by the number of days between restocking visits to calculate average daily sales. This metric will help you determine which machines are performing well and which may need adjustments (e.g., a change in location or products).

2. Monitoring Expenses

   Your expenses can vary depending on factors such as the type of machine you operate, the location, and the cost of your inventory. Common expenses include:

   o **Product costs:** The cost of purchasing snacks, drinks, or other items that you stock in your machine.
   o **Restocking and transportation costs:** Fuel and travel expenses incurred during restocking visits.
   o **Commissions or rent:** Payments to property owners who allow you to place your machines on their premises. This may be a percentage of sales (usually 5-20%) or a flat monthly rental fee.
   o **Maintenance and repairs:** Costs associated with maintaining or repairing your machines. For example, if a payment system malfunctions or a part needs replacing, you'll need to factor these expenses into your budget.
   o **Utilities:** For refrigerated vending machines, electricity costs should also be considered.

3. Profit Margins

   Once you have a clear picture of your sales and expenses, you can calculate your profit margins. To do this, subtract your total expenses from your total revenue, then divide by your total revenue to find your profit margin percentage.

For example:
- **Revenue:** $1,000
- **Expenses:** $600 (inventory, transportation, commissions, etc.)
- **Profit:** $400
- **Profit margin:** ($400 ÷ $1,000) x 100 = 40%

A healthy vending machine business typically has a profit margin of 30-50%. If your margins are lower than this, it's time to evaluate your expenses and pricing strategy to ensure you're maximizing profitability.

8.2 Reinvesting in Your Business

Once you've started generating a steady profit from your vending machines, it's essential to reinvest a portion of your earnings back into your business to ensure continued growth. Reinvestment can take many forms, including purchasing additional machines, upgrading existing machines, or exploring new product offerings.

1. **Expanding Your Fleet of Machines**
   One of the most straightforward ways to grow your vending machine business is by purchasing additional machines. By reinvesting profits into new machines, you can scale your business and increase your revenue potential. Before purchasing additional machines, consider the following:

   - **Location:** Have you identified more high-traffic locations where you can place additional machines? Expanding to new, profitable locations will maximize your investment.

- **Product variety:** Consider adding different types of machines (e.g., healthy vending machines, combination machines, or specialty vending machines) to appeal to a broader customer base.
- **Financing options:** If you're reinvesting profits, you can grow slowly and steadily without taking on debt. However, if you want to scale faster, you may explore financing options such as business loans to purchase more machines upfront.

2. **Upgrading Existing Machines**

If you're operating older vending machines, upgrading them to newer models with modern features can boost sales and improve operational efficiency. Here are a few reasons to consider upgrading your machines:

- **Payment options:** Modern machines often come equipped with card readers and mobile payment options like Apple Pay or Google Wallet. Offering cashless payment options can significantly increase sales, as many consumers no longer carry cash.
- **Energy efficiency:** Newer machines tend to be more energy-efficient, especially refrigerated drink machines. By upgrading, you can lower your electricity costs and reduce your environmental footprint.
- **Remote monitoring:** Machines with remote monitoring features allow you to track inventory levels, sales data, and machine performance from your computer or smartphone. This feature can save you time and money by helping you restock more efficiently and respond to maintenance issues faster.

3. Diversifying Product Offerings
   Reinvesting in your business doesn't always mean adding more machines. You can also grow by diversifying the products you offer in your existing machines. Expanding your product range to include seasonal items, healthier options, or specialty products can attract new customers and increase sales. For example:
   - o In an office building, offering coffee or energy drinks alongside snacks could boost morning sales.
   - o In a gym, stocking low-calorie, high-protein snacks could appeal to fitness-focused customers.

Keeping your product selection fresh and exciting will encourage repeat business and help your machines stand out from competitors.

8.3 Expanding Your Fleet of Machines

As your business grows, expanding your fleet of vending machines is a natural next step. This allows you to increase your revenue potential by operating multiple machines in various high-traffic locations. Here's how to scale your business efficiently:

1. Evaluating Your Best Locations
   Before expanding, analyze your current locations and identify which are generating the most revenue. Successful locations often share common characteristics:
   - o High foot traffic
   - o Strong demand for the products you offer
   - o Minimal competition from other vending machines or nearby food options

Once you've identified your most profitable locations, use that knowledge to find similar spots for new machines. For example, if your machines are doing well in gyms, look for more fitness centers or health clubs in your area.

2. Adding Different Types of Machines
Expanding your fleet doesn't always mean adding the same types of machines. You can diversify your business by adding different types of vending machines that cater to different customer needs:
   o **Healthy vending machines:** These are ideal for locations like gyms, schools, and hospitals, where consumers are more likely to seek out nutritious options.
   o **Specialty vending machines:** Machines that offer unique products like phone chargers, hygiene items, or travel essentials can be highly profitable in locations like airports, bus stations, or shopping malls.

By diversifying the types of machines you operate, you can capture different markets and reduce your reliance on any single location or product category.

3. Managing Multiple Machines
As you add more machines to your fleet, managing them efficiently becomes increasingly important. Here are some tips for handling the logistics of multiple machines:
   o **Create restocking routes:** If you have machines in various locations, plan your restocking routes to minimize travel time and fuel costs. Group machines in the same area and restock them on the same trip.
   o **Hire help if needed:** As your fleet grows, you may find it challenging to manage everything on your own.

Consider hiring part-time or full-time staff to help with restocking, maintenance, and customer service.

o **Use technology to streamline operations:** Remote monitoring systems and inventory tracking software can help you stay on top of sales, stock levels, and maintenance needs across multiple machines. This technology will save you time and help you manage your growing business more effectively.

CHAPTER 9:

DIGITAL MARKETING FOR VENDING MACHINES

In today's business environment, digital marketing is essential for growing your vending machine business. By creating an online presence and using digital tools, you can promote your machines, build brand awareness, and even secure more profitable locations. In this chapter, we'll explore how to build an effective digital marketing strategy, including how to utilize social media, SEO, email marketing, and paid advertising to grow your vending machine business.

9.1 Building an Online Presence for Your Business

An online presence is crucial for any business, including vending machine operators. It helps you establish credibility, showcase your products and services, and attract potential partners or property owners who might want to host your vending machines. Here's how to create a solid online presence:

1. Create a Professional Website
   Your website is the digital hub of your business. It's where potential partners, clients, and customers can learn more about your vending services, view the types of machines you offer, and reach out for inquiries. Here are a few essential elements for your website:
   - **About Page:** Share the story behind your business, your goals, and what sets you apart from other vending machine operators.

- **Services Page:** Detail the types of vending machines you provide (snack machines, healthy options, specialty vending, etc.) and the benefits of having vending machines in specific locations (e.g., increased convenience for employees or customers).
- **Contact Information:** Ensure your contact details (phone number, email, and social media links) are easily accessible. You can also add a contact form for inquiries.
- **Testimonials and Case Studies:** Include testimonials or case studies from property owners or customers who've benefited from your vending machines. Positive feedback will help build trust with new prospects.

If you don't have experience building websites, consider using easy website builders like Wix, Squarespace, or WordPress to get started. These platforms offer pre-designed templates and user-friendly tools to create a professional-looking site without the need for coding skills.

2. Leverage Social Media

   Social media platforms offer an excellent opportunity to engage with your audience, promote your vending machine business, and showcase your products and services. Here's how to effectively use popular platforms:
   - **Instagram:** Instagram is a highly visual platform, perfect for showcasing photos and videos of your vending machines in action. Share pictures of your machines, the locations where they're installed, the variety of products you offer, and customer interactions. You can also use Instagram Stories to provide behind-the-scenes content, such as restocking visits or new product additions.

- o **Facebook:** Facebook is a great platform for sharing updates about your business, engaging with potential clients (such as property owners or businesses interested in vending machines), and running ads. Create a business page where you can post regularly about new machines, locations, and promotional offers.
- o **LinkedIn:** If you're targeting corporate locations or professional partnerships (such as office buildings, gyms, or schools), LinkedIn can be a powerful tool. You can connect with property managers, facility coordinators, and business owners who might be interested in hosting your vending machines.
- o **YouTube**: If you're comfortable creating video content, YouTube is another way to build your brand. You could create instructional videos about running a vending machine business, share tips for keeping machines well-maintained, or provide case studies on the benefits of vending machines in specific locations.

3. Google My Business

    Google My Business is a free tool that allows your vending machine business to appear in local search results. This is especially important if you're targeting businesses, schools, or other organizations in your area. Setting up a Google My Business profile will help potential clients find you when they search for "vending machine services" in your region.
    Ensure your profile is complete with your business name, address, phone number, website link, and hours of operation. Encourage satisfied clients to leave reviews, as positive reviews will boost your credibility and visibility in search results.

9.2 Social Media Marketing for Local Engagement

Social media marketing isn't just about promoting your business; it's about building a community and engaging with your audience. By interacting with your followers and creating valuable content, you can attract more people to your business and keep your existing customers loyal.

1. **Engaging Content Ideas**
   Creating engaging content will help you stand out on social media and attract more followers. Here are some content ideas:
   - **Showcase your products:** Post pictures of the snacks, drinks, or specialty items in your vending machines. Highlight any new products or seasonal offerings to keep your audience interested.
   - **Behind-the-scenes content:** Share behind-the-scenes footage of restocking your machines, maintaining them, or adding new products. This gives your audience a glimpse into the inner workings of your business and builds trust.
   - **Customer testimonials:** Feature reviews or testimonials from satisfied clients who have vending machines in their offices or properties.
   - **Educational posts:** Provide tips and advice about the vending machine business, such as how to choose the right locations or the benefits of healthy vending options.
   - **Promotions and discounts:** Run promotions or offer limited-time discounts to encourage businesses to contact you about installing a vending machine.

2. Local Hashtags
   Using local hashtags can help you reach people in your area who are looking for vending machine services. For example, if you operate in New York, you could use hashtags like #NewYorkBusiness, #NYCoffice, or #HealthyVendingNYC. Research which hashtags are popular in your community to boost local engagement.

3. Collaborate with Local Influencers
   Partnering with local influencers can be a great way to promote your vending machines, especially if you're focusing on niche markets like gyms or health-conscious locations. For instance, you could collaborate with fitness influencers who frequent the gym where your vending machine is located, and they can post about your products and services.

9.3 SEO and Local Search Optimization

Search engine optimization (SEO) is the process of improving your website's ranking on search engines like Google. By optimizing your website and content for relevant search terms, you can attract more traffic to your site and generate leads for your vending machine business.

1. Local SEO for Vending Machines
   Local SEO is especially important if your goal is to attract businesses, property managers, or organizations in your area. Here's how to optimize your website for local search:
   - o **Include local keywords:** Use keywords that include your location, such as "vending machines in [City]" or "vending machine services near [City]." These keywords will help your website appear in search results when

potential clients look for vending machine providers in their area.

o **Optimize your Google My Business profile:** As mentioned earlier, ensure your Google My Business profile is complete and accurate. Encourage satisfied clients to leave reviews, as positive reviews can boost your local SEO ranking.

o **Add location-specific content:** Create blog posts or pages on your website that focus on specific locations or services. For example, you could write about the benefits of having vending machines in corporate offices in your city or highlight the demand for healthy vending machines in local schools.

2. On-Page SEO Tips

In addition to local SEO, optimizing your website's overall content is important for ranking higher on search engines. Here are a few on-page SEO tips:

o **Use relevant keywords:** Research and include keywords that potential clients might search for, such as "vending machine business," "vending machine leasing," or "healthy snack vending."

o **Optimize meta descriptions and titles:** Make sure your website pages have clear, concise meta descriptions and titles that include relevant keywords.

o **Use high-quality images:** Add images of your vending machines and products, and include descriptive alt text for each image to improve SEO.

o **Create high-quality content:** Regularly post blog articles or updates that provide value to your audience, such as tips on managing vending machines, the importance of offering healthy options, or case studies on successful machine placements.

9.4 Leveraging Email Marketing and Paid Ads

Email marketing and paid advertising can help you reach potential clients who are interested in placing vending machines at their locations. Here's how to get started:

1. **Email Marketing Campaigns**
   Email marketing is an effective way to stay in touch with potential clients and keep them updated on your business. Here's how to build an email marketing campaign:

   o **Build an email list:** Collect email addresses from businesses, property managers, or organizations that have shown interest in vending machine services. You can add a sign-up form to your website or ask for emails during inquiries.

   o **Send regular updates:** Share valuable content, such as new vending machine options, special promotions, or tips for increasing employee satisfaction with vending services. Keep your emails informative and relevant to your audience's needs.

   o **Personalize your emails:** Use the recipient's name and tailor your message to their specific needs. For example, if you're emailing an office manager, highlight the benefits of offering snacks and drinks to employees without needing to leave the office.

2. **Running Paid Ads**
   Paid advertising can be a great way to reach potential clients who may not have found your business through organic search or social media. Here are two paid ad options:

o **Google Ads:** Google Ads allows you to target people searching for vending machine services in your area. For example, you can create ads that appear when someone searches for "vending machines for office buildings" or "healthy vending machines near me."

o **Facebook and Instagram Ads:** Social media ads on platforms like Facebook and Instagram can be targeted based on location, interests, and demographics. You can create ads that target business owners or property managers in your area, offering them an incentive to contact you about installing a vending machine.

CHAPTER 10:

TAKING CARE OF YOUR MACHINES

Maintaining your vending machines is essential for keeping them running smoothly and maximizing their lifespan. Proper maintenance not only ensures that your machines remain operational but also helps you avoid costly repairs and downtime, which can lead to lost sales. In this chapter, we'll discuss the importance of regular maintenance, troubleshooting common issues, and when to consider upgrading your machines.

10.1 Regular Maintenance and Cleaning

Routine maintenance is the key to keeping your vending machines in excellent working condition. Just like any other piece of equipment, vending machines require regular upkeep to function efficiently and provide a positive customer experience.

1. Cleaning the Exterior
   Keeping the exterior of your machines clean and presentable is important for attracting customers. Dirty or grimy machines can deter potential users and give off a bad impression. During each restocking visit, take a few minutes to wipe down the exterior of your machines. Focus on areas like the display window, payment system, and product dispensing area. Regularly clean off fingerprints, dust, and any food or drink spills.

2. Cleaning the Interior
   The interior of your machine should also be cleaned regularly, especially if it dispenses food or drinks. Here's how to ensure the inside stays clean:
   - **Product shelves:** Remove and clean the product shelves or trays. This prevents debris or spills from accumulating and ensures that products are dispensed cleanly.
   - **Coin and bill acceptors:** Clean the coin and bill acceptors to prevent jams and ensure smooth transactions. Dust and debris can build up inside these components, causing issues with payments.
   - **Refrigeration units:** If your vending machine has a refrigeration unit, clean the condenser coils and check that the refrigeration system is functioning correctly. This ensures that drinks or perishable items stay fresh and that the unit doesn't overheat.

3. Preventing Jams and Misdispensing
   Jams occur when a product gets stuck in the machine and doesn't drop into the collection bin. Not only does this frustrate customers, but it can also lead to product damage and lost sales. Regularly check the dispensing mechanism for any signs of wear or obstruction. Adjust product placement on the shelves to ensure items are loaded correctly and that the vending mechanism can smoothly push them out.
   You can also reduce jams by ensuring that products are the right size for the machine. Overfilling shelves or using packages that are too large or awkwardly shaped for the machine can increase the risk of jams.

10.2 Troubleshooting Common Issues

Even with regular maintenance, vending machines can sometimes encounter problems. Here are some of the most common issues and how to troubleshoot them:

1. Payment System Malfunctions
   One of the most frustrating problems for both you and your customers is when the payment system fails. Whether the machine refuses to accept coins, bills, or credit cards, payment malfunctions can lead to lost sales and unhappy customers. Here's how to address this issue:

   o **Coin and bill jams:** If coins or bills are getting stuck, remove any debris or objects that may be blocking the path. Check the coin mechanism and bill acceptor for signs of wear or damage, and replace them if necessary.
   o **Card reader issues:** If your machine accepts credit or debit cards, make sure the card reader is functioning properly. If it's not, check the connection between the card reader and the machine's main control board. If the reader is damaged, you may need to replace it.
   o **Power issues:** If the machine is not powering on or if the payment system isn't responding, check the machine's power supply and ensure all electrical connections are secure.

2. Product Not Dispensing Properly
   Occasionally, products may not dispense as intended, either due to a jam or a mechanical failure. This is especially common with bulkier items or those placed incorrectly on the shelves. Here's how to resolve this issue:

o **Product placement:** Ensure that products are loaded correctly and that they fit within the shelf's space. Overfilling the shelves can lead to jams or blockages.
o **Vending mechanism:** Check the vending mechanism to ensure it's not obstructed. If you notice any parts that are worn out or broken, replace them to prevent future issues.
o **Temperature-related issues:** For refrigerated machines, improper cooling can cause drinks to stick together or freeze, making it difficult for them to dispense properly. Make sure the temperature is set appropriately, and check the refrigeration system regularly.

3. Refrigeration Problems

For machines that offer cold drinks or other perishable items, refrigeration issues can be particularly costly. If your vending machine is not keeping products cold, it can lead to spoiled items and lost revenue.

o **Check the thermostat:** Ensure that the thermostat is set to the correct temperature. If the temperature is too high, products may not cool properly.
o **Inspect the condenser coils:** Dirty condenser coils can cause the refrigeration system to overheat and malfunction. Clean the coils regularly to prevent overheating.
o **Fan motor problems:** If the fan motor is faulty, air may not circulate properly, causing the temperature inside the machine to rise. Check the fan motor for signs of wear and replace it if necessary.

10.3 Upgrading and Modernizing Your Machines

As your vending machine business grows, you may want to consider upgrading or modernizing your machines to improve efficiency and increase sales. Upgrading can include adding new features, replacing outdated machines, or investing in more energy-efficient models.

1. **Adding Cashless Payment Options**
   With the growing trend of cashless transactions, offering cashless payment options can significantly boost your sales. Many customers prefer to pay using credit cards, debit cards, or mobile payment systems like Apple Pay or Google Wallet. If your current machines only accept cash, consider upgrading to a card reader or a cashless payment system.
   Adding cashless payment options can:
   - o Attract more customers who prefer to pay electronically.
   - o Increase the average purchase size, as customers tend to spend more when paying with cards.
   - o Reduce the amount of cash you need to handle during restocking visits.

2. **Energy-Efficient Machines**
   Upgrading to energy-efficient machines can save you money on electricity costs, especially if you operate refrigerated drink machines. Look for machines with energy-saving features such as LED lighting, low-power refrigeration units, and automatic sleep modes that reduce energy consumption during off-peak hours. Energy-efficient machines not only save you money but also appeal to eco-conscious customers and businesses that want to reduce their environmental impact.

3. **Remote Monitoring and Smart Vending**
Investing in modern vending machines with remote monitoring capabilities can streamline your operations and improve efficiency. Smart vending machines allow you to:
   - o **Monitor inventory levels remotely:** This helps you plan restocking visits more efficiently and avoid stockouts.
   - o **Track sales data in real-time:** Knowing which products are selling well allows you to adjust your product offerings and maximize profits.
   - o **Receive maintenance alerts:** Remote monitoring systems can send alerts if the machine malfunctions, allowing you to address issues before they lead to significant downtime or lost sales.

4. **Updating Machine Appearance**
Appearance matters when it comes to vending machines. A machine that looks outdated or poorly maintained may discourage customers from using it. Consider upgrading the exterior of your machines with new branding, fresh decals, or sleek, modern designs to make them more appealing. If you're working with corporate clients or high-end locations, investing in machines with a polished, professional appearance can enhance your business image.

10.4 Handling Customer Issues and Refunds

Even with the best maintenance practices, problems may occasionally arise. To keep customers happy and maintain your reputation, it's essential to have a system in place for handling customer complaints and providing refunds.

1. Posting Clear Contact Information
   Make it easy for customers to reach you if they experience any issues with your machine. Clearly post your contact information (email, phone number, or website) on the machine itself. Include instructions for how customers can request a refund or report a problem.
2. Offering Prompt Refunds
   Refunds are an important part of maintaining customer satisfaction. If a product doesn't dispense correctly, or if a machine malfunctions, make sure to issue refunds promptly. Many vending operators choose to offer refunds via mail, email, or mobile payment apps like Venmo or PayPal.
3. Responding to Complaints Quickly
   When customers report an issue, respond quickly to resolve the problem. Whether it's a stuck product, a payment error, or a machine malfunction, addressing the issue in a timely manner shows that you value customer satisfaction and are committed to providing excellent service.

CHAPTER 11:

RULES, REGULATIONS, AND COMPLIANCE

Running a vending machine business involves more than just placing machines and stocking them with products. To operate legally and protect yourself from potential liabilities, it's essential to comply with local regulations, obtain the necessary permits, and follow health and safety standards. In this chapter, we'll cover the key rules, permits, and insurance requirements you need to be aware of to keep your vending machine business compliant with the law.

11.1 Permits and Licensing Requirements

Before you can legally operate your vending machines, you may need to obtain certain permits or licenses, depending on your location and the types of products you plan to sell. Local governments often regulate vending machines to ensure public safety and collect taxes on sales. Here's an overview of the most common permits and licenses required for vending machines:

1. Business License
   In most regions, you will need a general business license to operate a vending machine business. A business license allows you to legally conduct business in your city, county, or state. The requirements for obtaining a business license vary depending on your location, but generally, you'll need to:
   - o **Register your business:** This may include registering as a sole proprietor, partnership, LLC, or corporation.

o **Pay a licensing fee:** Licensing fees can range from $50 to several hundred dollars, depending on the jurisdiction.

2. Vending Machine License
    Many local governments require operators to obtain a specific vending machine license or permit for each machine they place in a public or private location. This permit ensures that your machines comply with local regulations and that you are properly registered with the authorities. The cost of a vending machine license is typically modest but may vary based on the number of machines you operate.

3. Health Permits
    If you're selling food or beverages through your vending machines, you may be required to obtain a health permit from your local health department. Health permits are particularly important if you're selling perishable items, such as sandwiches, yogurt, or fresh fruit. Health inspections ensure that the food you sell is safe for consumption and that your vending machines meet sanitation and refrigeration standards. When applying for a health permit, be prepared for an inspection of your vending machines to ensure they meet local health and safety regulations. The health department may check:
    o **Refrigeration systems:** Ensure that refrigerated machines are keeping perishable items at safe temperatures.
    o **Sanitation:** Machines must be clean and free from pests or contamination.
    o **Food labeling:** Packaged foods should be properly labeled with ingredients and expiration dates.

4. Sales Tax Permit
   In most states, you'll need to collect sales tax on the products you sell through your vending machines. To do this, you'll need to apply for a sales tax permit with your state's department of revenue. This permit allows you to collect and remit sales taxes to the state on a regular basis. Make sure you understand your state's sales tax requirements and set up a system for tracking and reporting sales tax from your vending machines.

11.2 Health and Safety Regulations

When operating a vending machine business, it's your responsibility to ensure that the products you sell are safe for customers. This is especially important if you're selling food and beverages. Local health departments and other regulatory agencies have guidelines in place to protect public health, and failing to comply with these regulations can result in fines or the suspension of your business license.

1. Food Safety Standards
   If you sell perishable items such as refrigerated drinks, sandwiches, or dairy products, your vending machines must meet strict food safety standards. This includes:
   - **Maintaining proper temperatures:** Refrigerated items should be kept at a temperature below 40°F (4°C) to prevent spoilage and the growth of harmful bacteria.
   - **Product rotation:** Ensure that perishable items are rotated regularly to avoid selling expired or spoiled products. Label products with expiration dates and remove them before they expire.
   - **Cleanliness:** Machines that dispense food and beverages must be cleaned regularly to prevent

         o contamination. Pay particular attention to the product dispensing area and any areas where customers come into contact with the machine.

    2. ADA Compliance
       The Americans with Disabilities Act (ADA) requires vending machines in public spaces to be accessible to individuals with disabilities. This means that customers with mobility impairments must be able to access and use the machine without difficulty. To ensure ADA compliance, your vending machines should meet the following guidelines:
         o **Reachability:** The machine's payment and dispensing mechanisms must be within reach of customers using wheelchairs or other mobility devices. Typically, the height of the operational controls should be between 15 and 48 inches from the floor.
         o **Accessibility of payment options:** Make sure that customers with disabilities can easily use the machine's payment systems, whether they're paying with cash, card, or mobile payments.

Failing to comply with ADA regulations can result in fines or lawsuits, so it's essential to make sure your machines are accessible to all customers.

11.3 Insurance and Liability

Running a vending machine business comes with certain risks, and it's important to protect yourself from potential liabilities. Insurance coverage can help shield you from financial losses in the event of accidents, theft, or equipment failure. Here are the most common types of insurance you should consider:

1. General Liability Insurance

   General liability insurance is a must-have for vending machine operators. This type of coverage protects your business in case someone is injured by your machine or claims that the machine caused damage. For example, if a customer is hurt while trying to retrieve a product or if your machine causes damage to the property where it's located, general liability insurance will cover legal fees, medical expenses, and damages.

2. Property Insurance

   Property insurance covers the cost of repairing or replacing your vending machines in the event they are damaged or destroyed by fire, vandalism, theft, or natural disasters. Since vending machines are valuable assets, it's important to have coverage that protects your investment. If one of your machines is damaged in a break-in, property insurance will cover the cost of repairs or replacement.

3. Product Liability Insurance

   If you sell food or beverages through your vending machines, product liability insurance can protect you from lawsuits related to foodborne illnesses or other health issues caused by the products you sell. For example, if a customer becomes ill after consuming an expired or contaminated item from your vending machine, product liability insurance will cover the legal costs and damages associated with the lawsuit.

4. Worker's Compensation Insurance

   If you hire employees to help you manage your vending machines (such as restocking or maintenance workers), you may be required to carry worker's compensation insurance.

This type of insurance provides coverage for medical expenses and lost wages if an employee is injured on the job. Requirements for worker's compensation insurance vary by state, so check with your local labor department to ensure compliance.

11.4 Staying Informed About Regulations

Regulations governing vending machines can vary from state to state and even between cities or counties. To avoid penalties, it's important to stay informed about the laws that apply to your business. Here are a few ways to stay up-to-date on regulations:

1. **Contact your local health department**
   They can provide information on food safety regulations and health permits specific to your area.
2. **Check with your state's department of revenue**
   They can provide guidance on sales tax collection and reporting.
3. **Consult with a business attorney**
   A lawyer who specializes in small business regulations can help ensure that you're in compliance with all local, state, and federal laws.

CHAPTER 12:

CONCLUSION

Congratulations! By now, you've learned the essential steps and strategies for building and growing a successful vending machine business. From understanding the basics of vending machines to selecting prime locations, stocking your machines, managing your finances, and leveraging digital marketing, you are well-equipped to launch and scale your venture.

12.1 Recap of Key Points

Let's take a moment to review the key takeaways from each chapter:

- **What is a Vending Machine?**
  You now understand the role that vending machines play in providing convenience to customers, offering everything from snacks and drinks to specialty items. The versatility of vending machines allows you to cater to various markets and customer preferences.

- **Why Start a Vending Machine Business?**
  The vending machine business offers numerous advantages, including low operating costs, passive income, scalability, and flexibility. You've learned how to assess the income potential of your machines and the benefits of expanding your business over time.

- Building a Business Plan

A solid business plan is essential for setting goals, identifying your target market, and outlining your financial projections. You've learned how to create a roadmap for success and how to budget for both short-term and long-term growth.

- **Picking the Right Vending Machines**
  Choosing the right type of vending machine depends on your target audience and location. Whether it's a snack machine, drink machine, combination machine, or specialty vending machine, you've gained insight into how to select the best option for your business.

- **Finding Good Locations**
  Location is key to your vending machine's success. You've learned how to identify high-traffic areas, negotiate with property owners, and analyze competition to maximize your machine's performance.

- **Stocking and Managing Your Machines**
  Stocking your machines with the right products is crucial for keeping customers satisfied and driving sales. You now know how to choose products based on customer preferences, create restocking schedules, and maintain the quality of your products.

- **Money Management and Growth**
  Proper financial management is vital for tracking revenue, managing expenses, and reinvesting in your business. You've learned how to scale your business by expanding your fleet of machines, upgrading equipment, and diversifying your product offerings.

- **Digital Marketing for Vending Machines**
  Digital marketing is a powerful tool for growing your vending machine business. From building an online presence to utilizing social media, SEO, email marketing, and paid ads, you've learned how to promote your business and attract potential clients and property owners.

- **Taking Care of Your Machines**
  Regular maintenance and troubleshooting help ensure that your machines remain operational and profitable. You've gained valuable tips on cleaning, preventing jams, handling payment issues, and upgrading your machines to improve efficiency.

- **Rules, Regulations, and Compliance**
  Running a legal and compliant vending machine business requires obtaining the necessary permits, following health and safety regulations, and securing insurance. You've learned how to protect your business from liabilities and ensure compliance with local laws.

12.2 Preparing for Your Vending Journey

As you prepare to embark on your vending machine business journey, keep in mind that success doesn't happen overnight. It takes time, effort, and careful planning to build a profitable business. The knowledge you've gained from this guide will serve as your foundation, but it's up to you to put that knowledge into action.

Here are a few final tips to help you get started:

1. **Start Small, Then Scale**

If you're new to the vending machine business, it's often best to start with one or two machines. This allows you to learn the ropes, test different products, and fine-tune your operations before expanding. Once you're confident in your ability to manage your machines effectively, you can begin scaling your business by adding more machines and exploring new locations.

2. Be Flexible and Adaptable

    The vending machine industry is constantly evolving, with new trends and customer preferences emerging over time. Stay flexible and be willing to adapt your business model as needed. Whether that means offering healthier products, upgrading your machines to accept cashless payments, or targeting new markets, staying ahead of the curve will help you remain competitive and profitable.

3. Focus on Customer Satisfaction

    Customer satisfaction is key to your success. Happy customers are more likely to return to your machines and spread the word about your business. Keep your machines clean, well-stocked, and in good working condition to provide the best possible experience for your customers.

4. Keep Learning

    The vending machine business offers endless opportunities for growth, and there's always more to learn. Continue educating yourself about industry trends, new technologies, and ways to improve your operations. Join vending machine associations, attend industry conferences, and network with other operators to stay informed and inspired.

12.3 Final Tips for Success

As you move forward, here are a few additional tips to help you achieve long-term success:

1. **Network with Other Business Owners**
   Building relationships with other local business owners can open doors to new locations and partnerships. Whether you're placing machines in office buildings, gyms, or schools, networking can help you expand your reach and grow your business.

2. **Monitor Your Machines Regularly**
   Even if your vending machines are running smoothly, it's important to check in on them regularly. Keep an eye on inventory levels, sales data, and machine performance to catch any issues early and prevent costly repairs or downtime.

3. **Track Your Progress**
   Set clear goals for your business and track your progress over time. By analyzing sales trends, customer preferences, and location performance, you'll be able to make data-driven decisions that drive growth and profitability.

4. **Stay Organized**
   As your business grows, staying organized is key to managing multiple machines, locations, and financial records. Use tools like spreadsheets, inventory management software, and financial tracking apps to streamline your operations and keep everything running smoothly.

12.4 Moving Forward

Starting a vending machine business is a rewarding venture that offers flexibility, passive income, and the potential for long-term growth. By following the steps outlined in this guide and staying focused on your goals, you can build a thriving business that serves your customers' needs while generating steady profits.

Remember, success in the vending machine industry requires patience, persistence, and a willingness to adapt. But with careful planning and hard work, you can turn your vending machine business into a profitable and scalable enterprise.

Best of luck on your journey to vending machine success!

www.ingramcontent.com/pod-product-compliance
Lightning Source LLC
Chambersburg PA
CBHW040223220526
45473CB00001B/99